THE BEST 50

MUSHROOM RECIPES

Barbara Karoff

BRISTOL PUBLISHING ENTERPRISES
San Leandro, California

Printed in the United States of America.

ISBN 1-55867-128-5

Cover design: Paredes Design Associates
Cover photography: John A. Benson
Food stylist: Suzanne Carreiro

ABOUT MUSHROOMS

Throughout the world there are over 10,000 varieties of mushrooms, and several dozen are available to us — fresh, dried or canned. Canned mushrooms, in general, are not rewarding.

MUSHROOM VARIETIES

Our most common mushroom is the fat, round and very familiar *white button* variety. Cultivated since the seventeenth century in France, it is available year-round in various sizes. The *brown button* is similar, just a different color.

Recently, various wild mushrooms, or to be specific, cultivated wild mushrooms, have become regular features in well-stocked produce departments. Most often available is the meaty, full-flavored *shiitake*, grown by the Japanese for 2,000 years and now widely grown in the United States. The *oyster* is a creamy white mushroom with a faint woodsy flavor. The huge brown *Portobello* (also known as *cremini*) is a meal in itself and is excellent grilled. The *chanterelle* is known for its apricot aroma. It has a thick stem and a big, wavy cap. The Japanese *enoki* (or *enokitake*) is a dainty cluster of tiny stems with small button caps and is best eaten raw. The famous and flavorful Italian *porcini* is sometimes available fresh, but is most often dried — this mushroom is called *cèpe* in France and Spain and *Steinpilze* in Germany. The dried variety keeps its flavor well. The *morel*, also a European import, is one of the few mushrooms that may be better dried than fresh. The *wood ear* (also called *black fungus*, *cloud ear* and *tree ear*), a dried mushroom, is imported from China. It has a woodsy flavor and an unusual crunchy texture, even after soaking and cooking.

Many other varieties are available occasionally, and more are showing up all the time. Try the new varieties. They each add their own distinctive flavor — and often texture as well.

Each recipe in this book calls for either fresh or dried mushrooms. Although different varieties produce different flavors and intensities, most are interchangeable. This is true of the recipes that follow, with the exception of those that call for dried mushrooms.

Wild mushrooms are often considerably more expensive than white and brown buttons. They also have a lot more flavor — only a few added to a dish create a noticeable and delightful difference. Mushrooms vary in intensity from one batch to the next, so alter the amount used if the flavor is stronger or milder than expected.

When "wild" mushrooms are called for in this book, "wild" relates *specifically* to the cultivated wild mushrooms now available in some markets. Do not take to the woods to gather mushrooms on your own. It's a tricky, and possibly lethal, business for anyone who is not extremely skilled and knowledgeable on the subject. Instead, talk your local produce buyer into offering more varieties.

PURCHASING AND CLEANING MUSHROOMS

Whether mushroom caps are open or closed makes little difference. The flavor of those with open caps tends to be more robust; the flavor of those with closed caps is more delicate. When purchasing fresh mushrooms, avoid any that are dark, wrinkled, slimy or bruised.

All mushrooms are fragile, highly perishable and should be used as soon as possible after purchasing. Do not store in a plastic bag.

Dried mushrooms must always be soaked in hot (not boiling) liquid for 30 minutes before using. The liquid can be water, stock or wine, depending on the recipe, and the liquid is frequently added to the dish. If not, save it for another use. Because dried mushrooms often contain sand and grit, the soaking liquid must be strained before using. A paper coffee filter is ideal for this step (no fuss, no muss and throw it away when you are through), but you can also use a triple thickness of damp cheesecloth. After soaking, the mushrooms must be rinsed carefully in warm water and then squeezed dry. Discard any tough stems.

All mushrooms — especially wild and dried varieties — must be cleaned well before using.

The specially designed, soft-bristled mushroom brush is ideal for cleaning fresh mushrooms. Dampen the brush, if necessary, and quickly brush the caps and stems to remove all clinging dirt.

Trim the stem ends and discard stems that are large and woody.

If you do not have a mushroom brush, a damp towel works well. The important thing is not to immerse fresh mushrooms in water, or even to clean them under running water, because they act like sponges and will then impart a watery flavor to the dish.

TIPS AND HELPFUL HINTS

- Fresh or dried, mushrooms are low in calories and cholesterol.
- One pound fresh mushrooms equals about 6 cups sliced. Three ounces dried mushrooms equals about 1 pound fresh.
- Use a food processor to chop large amounts of mushrooms. Pulse on and off and do not do too many at once.
- Recipes often call for sautéing mushrooms before adding them to a dish, even if they will be cooked again. This is to cook away excess moisture. The first cooking also develops the mushrooms' full, rich flavor.
- In recipes that call for dry white wine, try using dry vermouth. Since it is fortified, it keeps, unrefrigerated, almost indefinitely.

MUSHROOM-ALMOND PATÉ

Makes 1 cup

Almonds and mushrooms are a subtle and just about perfect combination in this appetizer spread. Serve with lightly toasted baguette slices.

½ cup almonds, with skin
2 tbs. butter
1 shallot, chopped
1 clove garlic, chopped
½ lb. fresh mushrooms, sliced
pinch dried thyme
salt and pepper
1 tbs. canola oil

Preheat oven to 350°. In a shallow pan, toast almonds for about 10 minutes. Cool. In a medium skillet, melt butter and sauté shallot, garlic, mushrooms, thyme, salt and pepper until shallots are soft and mixture is quite dry. In a food processor or blender, grind almonds to a smooth paste. With motor running, add oil and process until creamy. Add mushroom mixture and process until smooth. Place in a 1-cup crock and serve warm or at room temperature.

CURRIED MUSHROOM PATÉ

Makes 1½ cups

A scrambled egg is the surprise ingredient in this elegant paté.

½ lb. fresh mushrooms, sliced
2 tbs. butter
½ tbs. lemon juice
dash Tabasco Sauce
1 tsp. curry powder, or to taste

7 tbs. butter, softened
1 egg, scrambled in 1 tbs. butter
¼ cup finely grated cheddar
  cheese
salt and pepper

In a large skillet, sauté mushrooms in 2 tbs. butter. Add lemon juice and cook for 5 minutes, stirring frequently. In a food processor or blender, puree mushrooms and sautéing liquid. Cool slightly. Add Tabasco, curry powder and 7 tbs. butter. Transfer to a bowl and stir in scrambled egg, cheese, salt and pepper. Mix well to break up chunks of egg. Spoon into a 1½- or 2-cup crock and refrigerate. Bring to room temperature before serving.

MUSHROOM APPETIZER PUFFS

Makes about 30

These light and airy little puffs are delicious served warm.

1½ cups water
½ cup butter
1½ cups all-purpose flour
½ tsp. salt

6 eggs
1½ cups grated Swiss cheese
1½ cups finely chopped fresh
  mushrooms

Preheat oven to 400° and lightly grease a baking sheet. In a medium saucepan, bring water and butter to a boil. Add flour and salt all at once. Beat with a wooden spoon until mixture forms a ball. Remove from heat and beat in eggs, one at a time. Mix well. Add cheese and mushrooms and beat to combine. Drop by teaspoonfuls onto baking sheet and bake until golden and puffy, about 20 minutes. Cooking time will vary, depending on size. Serve warm.

MUSHROOM APPETIZER TARTS

Makes 6-12 small tarts or 2 large tarts

Use your favorite recipe or buy uncooked shells in the dairy case.

1 recipe for 2-crust pie pastry, or
  prepared pastry shells, unbaked
2 tbs. canola oil
1 lb. fresh mushrooms, sliced
2 small leeks, white part only,
  thinly sliced

2 cloves garlic, minced
¼ cup minced oil-packed
  sun-dried tomatoes
¼ cup dry white wine
6 oz. goat cheese, softened

Preheat oven to 350°. On a floured surface, roll pastry to desired size (or unwrap prepared shells) and place in muffin tins or pie pans. Bake for 12 to 15 minutes or until golden. Remove to a rack to cool.

Heat oil in a skillet and sauté mushrooms, leeks and garlic until soft. Add tomatoes and wine and cook until mixture is quite dry. Spoon into tart shells and crumble goat cheese over tops. Set filled shells on a baking sheet and place under the broiler until cheese bubbles. Serve warm.

MUSHROOMS À LA GRECQUE

Makes about 20

This Greek-style appetizer is always well received.

3 cups chicken stock
1 cup dry white wine
¾ cup olive oil
½ cup lemon juice
6 sprigs fresh parsley
4 cloves garlic, chopped

½ tsp. dried thyme
10 peppercorns
salt
1 lb. small fresh white or
   brown button mushrooms

In a medium saucepan, simmer stock, wine, oil, lemon juice, parsley, garlic, thyme, peppercorns and salt for 45 minutes. Strain and return to pan. Bring to a simmer and add mushrooms. Cover and simmer for 10 minutes. Transfer mushrooms to a shallow dish and cover with marinade. Refrigerate, covered, for at least 4 hours. Remove from marinade and serve with toothpicks.

STUFFED MUSHROOMS

Makes about 20

Try these as a side dish with steak, hamburger or broiled chicken.

1 lb. medium-sized fresh white button mushrooms
1 tbs. butter
1 small onion, minced
¼ cup Madeira or dry sherry
3 tbs. heavy cream
¼ cup freshly grated Parmesan cheese
½ tsp. dried thyme
¼-½ cup dry breadcrumbs
2 tbs. butter

Preheat oven to 375°. Remove stems from mushrooms. Set caps aside and finely chop stems. In a small skillet, melt 1 tbs. butter and sauté mushroom stems and onion until soft and dry. Mix in Madeira (or sherry), cream, Parmesan, thyme and just enough breadcrumbs to take up the moisture.

Spoon stuffing into mushroom caps and arrange in a single layer in a shallow baking dish. Place a small dab of butter on each mushroom and pour about $\frac{1}{4}$ inch of water into the dish. Cover tightly with foil and bake for 25 minutes. Serve warm.

EXOTIC MUSHROOMS

Servings 4-6

*Saffron, ginger, mushrooms and leeks combine to create
an unusual first course. Serve over hot, buttered toast.*

8 small leeks, white part only,
 thinly sliced
3 tbs. butter
1½ lb. fresh mushrooms,
 quartered
1 cup chicken stock

½ tsp. brown sugar
⅛ tsp. saffron threads, crushed
 with a spoon
½ tsp. grated ginger root
3 tbs. butter, softened
3 tbs. all-purpose flour

Sauté leeks in butter until they begin to wilt. Add mushrooms, toss
to combine and cook for 3 minutes. Combine stock, sugar, saffron
and ginger; pour over vegetables. Cover. Simmer for 2 minutes.
Combine 3 tbs. butter and flour and gradually add to vegetables,
stirring as mixture thickens.

CHEESY MUSHROOM EMPANADAS

Makes 20

Serve these empanadas warm for a special treat.

1 recipe *Cream Cheese Pastry*, page 17
3 tbs. butter
1 lb. fresh mushrooms, finely chopped
salt and pepper
3 green onions, finely chopped
½ tsp. dried thyme
1 cup finely grated Swiss cheese

Prepare *Cream Cheese Pastry*. Set aside. Preheat oven to 450°. In a large skillet, melt butter and sauté mushrooms until soft. Add salt, pepper, green onions and thyme; cook until onions are wilted and mixture is quite dry. Remove from heat. When cool, add cheese; combine well. Place a spoonful on one side of each pastry round. Fold over to form a half-circle and seal with the tines of a fork. Bake filled empanadas for 8 to 10 minutes or until nicely browned.

SPICY MUSHROOM EMPANADAS

Makes 20

*Empanadas are a popular South American treat.
They freeze well, either baked or unbaked.*

1 recipe *Cream Cheese Pastry*,
 follows
3 tbs. butter
1 lb. fresh mushrooms, finely
 chopped
salt and pepper

1 tbs. minced fresh cilantro
2 cloves garlic, minced
3 tbs. chopped roasted red
 pepper or pimiento
⅓ cup half-and-half
1 egg yolk

Prepare *Cream Cheese Pastry*. Set aside. Preheat oven to 450°. In a large skillet, melt butter and sauté mushrooms until soft. Add salt, pepper, cilantro, garlic and red pepper and cook for 2 minutes. Combine half-and-half and egg yolk and add to skillet. Stir to combine, remove from heat and cool. Place a spoonful on one ide of each pastry round. Fold over to form a half-circle and seal with the tines of a fork. Bake empanadas for 8 to 10 minutes or until nicely browned.

CREAM CHEESE PASTRY

3 oz. cream cheese, softened
½ cup butter, softened
generous dash Tabasco Sauce
salt
¼ cup freshly grated Parmesan cheese
1 cup all-purpose flour

Combine cream cheese, butter, Tabasco and salt in a food processor or by hand. Add cheese and flour and combine well. Chill dough for 30 minutes before rolling to ⅛-inch thickness. Cut into 3-inch rounds. Makes twenty 3-inch pastries.

CREAM OF MUSHROOM SOUP WITH WHITE WINE

Servings 4

This flavorful soup is a taste treat.

1 lb. fresh mushrooms, thickly sliced
1 cup dry white wine
¼ cup butter
1 clove garlic, minced
1 carrot, peeled and sliced
1 stalk celery, sliced
1 onion, sliced
3 cups milk
salt and pepper
½ tsp. mace
1½ cups half-and-half
¼ cup minced fresh parsley

Place mushrooms and wine in a medium saucepan. Bring to a boil, reduce heat and simmer, covered, for 15 minutes. Set aside.

In a large skillet, melt butter and sauté garlic, carrot, celery and onion until soft. Stir in milk, salt, pepper and mace. Simmer for 10 minutes, but do not boil. Puree in a food mill or food processor and return to pan. Puree mushrooms and wine in food mill or food processor and combine the two purees. Add half-and-half and carefully heat just to the boiling point. Stir in parsley and serve.

COLD MUSHROOM SOUP

Servings 4-6

This cool and creamy soup is perfect for a summer meal.

¾ lb. fresh mushrooms
2 tbs. olive oil
2 tbs. minced shallots
1 tsp. lemon juice
3 cups chicken stock
1 tbs. minced fresh parsley
½ cup half-and-half
2 egg yolks
1 tsp. paprika
salt and pepper

Slice mushrooms, reserving several slices for garnish. Place oil in a medium saucepan and sauté shallots and mushrooms (except for reserved slices) until soft. Add lemon juice, stock and parsley and simmer for 30 minutes. Puree soup in a food mill or food processor and return to pan.

In a small bowl, whisk together half-and-half, egg yolks and paprika. Stir in ½ cup hot soup. Add egg yolk mixture to soup in pan. Cook and stir for 3 minutes. Add salt and pepper. Chill. Serve cold, garnished with sliced mushrooms.

CHICKEN AND MUSHROOM SOUP

Servings 4-6

*The flavor of mushrooms really comes through in
this delicious and substantial soup.*

3 tbs. butter
1/3 cup finely chopped onion
1 lb. fresh mushrooms, sliced
4 cups chicken stock
1 1/2 cups half-and-half
1/2 cup dry white wine

salt
1/2 tsp. Tabasco Sauce
2 1/2 cups finely diced cooked
  chicken
1/4 tsp. dried tarragon

In a large pot, melt butter and sauté onion until soft. Add mushrooms and cook for 10 minutes. Add stock, half-and-half and wine and stir over medium heat until mixture comes to a boil. Reduce heat and simmer for 10 minutes. Add salt, Tabasco, chicken and tarragon and continue to simmer for 15 minutes.

MUSHROOM SOUP
(ZUPPA DI FUNGHI)

Servings 6

This quickly prepared soup is an Italian favorite.

2 slices lean bacon or pancetta,
   minced
2 tbs. minced fresh parsley
1 lb. fresh mushrooms, thinly
   sliced

6 cups chicken stock
salt and pepper
1 egg, beaten
¼ cup freshly grated Parmesan
   cheese

In a medium skillet, sauté bacon and parsley until bacon is crisp. Add mushrooms and sauté until soft. In a medium saucepan, bring stock to a boil. Add mushroom mixture, salt and pepper. Simmer for 15 minutes. In a small bowl, combine beaten egg and cheese and divide mixture among 6 soup bowls. Ladle hot soup into bowls and serve at once.

ITALIAN MUSHROOM SOUP

Servings 4

Dried porcini mushrooms make this soup rich and earthy.

1½ cups hot water
¾ oz. dried porcini mushrooms
1 tbs. butter
1 clove garlic, pressed
½ onion, thinly sliced
½ lb. fresh mushrooms, thinly sliced
½ cup dry white wine
4 cups beef stock
salt and pepper
4 thick slices firm-textured bread, toasted
¾ cup freshly grated Parmesan cheese

In a small bowl, pour hot water over dried mushrooms and soak for 30 minutes. Strain through a paper coffee filter, reserving liquid. Rinse mushrooms, squeeze dry and chop coarsely.

In a medium saucepan, melt butter and sauté garlic and onion until soft. Add fresh mushrooms and sauté until pan juices evaporate. Add dried mushrooms, 1 cup soaking liquid and wine. Boil for 3 to 4 minutes. Reduce heat, add stock and simmer for 15 minutes. Add salt and pepper. To serve, place a slice of toast in each of 4 soup plates. Ladle soup over toast and top with Parmesan cheese.

MUSHROOM SOUP PROVENÇAL

Servings 4

This quick and easy-to-prepare soup is good either hot or cold.

2 slices firm-textured white bread
3½ cups chicken stock
¾ lb. fresh mushrooms, chopped
1 tbs. lemon juice
2 tbs. butter
2 cloves garlic, chopped
2 tsp. minced fresh parsley
salt and pepper
¼ tsp. freshly grated nutmeg
½ cup heavy cream, warmed

Soak bread in stock and set aside. In a medium saucepan, sprinkle mushrooms with lemon juice and sauté in butter for 2 minutes. Add garlic, parsley, salt, pepper and nutmeg and continue to simmer for 5 minutes. Squeeze stock from bread and stir bread into mushrooms. Add stock and simmer for 10 minutes. Puree soup in a blender or food processor and return to pan. Add warm cream and bring just to a boil.

POLISH FRESH MUSHROOM SOUP

Servings 6

Mushrooms are a popular favorite in Eastern Europe.

½ lb. fresh mushrooms, thickly
  sliced
3 tbs. butter
¼ tsp. crushed caraway seeds
½ tsp. sweet paprika

1 tbs. all-purpose flour
4 cups chicken stock
1 egg yolk
1 cup sour cream
fresh or dried dill to taste

In a large skillet, sauté mushrooms in butter with caraway seeds and paprika for 1 minute. Sprinkle with flour and stir to blend. Gradually add stock, stir well, reduce heat and simmer, covered, for 30 minutes.

In a small bowl, whisk together egg yolk, sour cream and dill. Add ½ cup hot broth, mix well and add to skillet. Stir to prevent curdling and do not allow to boil.

MUSHROOM BISQUE

Servings 4

Wild mushrooms elevate this soup to exquisite heights.

½ lb. fresh mushrooms
1 tbs. butter
½ onion, finely chopped
2 cups chicken stock
3 tbs. butter

3 tbs. all-purpose flour
2 cups half-and-half
salt and white pepper
dash Tabasco Sauce
1 tbs. dry sherry

Thickly slice 6 mushroom caps and sauté in 1 tbs. butter until soft; reserve for garnish. Finely chop remaining mushrooms. Simmer with onion and stock in a large pot for 30 minutes. In a medium saucepan, melt 3 tbs. butter. Whisk in flour, cook for 2 minutes without browning and whisk in half-and-half. Stir in mushroom mixture, salt, pepper, Tabasco and sherry. To serve, garnish each serving with reserved mushroom slices.

ENOKI AND SPINACH SALAD

Servings 6

The spindly-stemmed enoki mushrooms add more texture than taste — and a dramatic color contrast.

1½ lb. spinach, large stems removed
1 bag (3½ oz.) fresh enoki mushrooms
2 pears, ripe but firm
2 green onions, thinly sliced

DRESSING

¼ cup sugar
⅓ cup rice vinegar
pinch salt
3 tbs. olive oil

Tear spinach into bite-sized pieces. Trim stem ends from mushrooms, rinse and shake off excess moisture. Peel, core and slice pears. In a salad bowl, combine spinach, mushrooms, pears and green onions. Whisk dressing ingredients together until sugar is dissolved. Toss salad with dressing just to moisten.

CHINESE CHICKEN
AND MUSHROOM SALAD

Servings 4

This unusual salad makes a fine luncheon or supper dish.

Sesame-Soy Dressing, follows
2 cups snow peas
4 cups thickly sliced fresh mushrooms
2 cups thinly sliced celery
2 cans (8 oz. each) water chestnuts, drained and thinly sliced
2 cups shredded cooked chicken
lettuce

Prepare *Sesame-Soy Dressing* and set aside. Steam snow peas for 2 minutes and cool in cold water; do not overcook. Place mushrooms, celery, snow peas and water chestnuts in a large bowl and pour all of the dressing over vegetables. Cover and refrigerate for 2 hours. Drain vegetables and arrange with chicken on a lettuce-lined serving platter.

SESAME-SOY DRESSING

2 cloves garlic, pressed or minced
¾ cup canola or peanut oil
6 tbs. soy sauce
6 tbs. lemon juice
2 tbs. rice vinegar
2 tbs. grated ginger root
4 tsp. Dijon mustard
3 tbs. sesame seeds

Combine all ingredients.

MUSHROOM AND FENNEL SALAD

Servings 4-6

This salad can be made with celery if fennel is not available, or with a combination of the two.

VINAIGRETTE

1 clove garlic, pressed or minced
¼ tsp. salt
2 tbs. lemon juice
pinch crushed fennel seeds
4-5 tbs. olive oil

1 lb. fresh mushrooms, thinly sliced
1 bulb fennel, trimmed, quartered and thinly sliced
2 tbs. minced fresh parsley
salt and pepper
½ lb. mixed greens
4 oz. feta cheese, crumbled

In a medium bowl, combine all vinaigrette ingredients.

Place mushrooms in another bowl and add 2 tbs. vinaigrette, coating well. Cover and refrigerate for 1 hour. Add fennel and parsley to remaining vinaigrette. Season with salt and pepper. Set aside. To serve, combine mushrooms and fennel and spoon over a bed of mixed greens. Sprinkle with feta cheese.

BISTRO SALAD

Servings 8

Serve this winter salad on a bed of romaine or butter lettuce.

DRESSING

½ cup olive oil
¼ cup sherry wine vinegar

½ tsp. salt
½ tsp. dried tarragon

---

1 lb. fresh mushrooms, sliced
3 small heads endive, thinly sliced
1 cup thinly sliced celery

lettuce leaves
1½ cups coarsely grated Swiss cheese
2 tbs. minced chives

Whisk together dressing ingredients. In a bowl, combine mushrooms, endive and celery with dressing to moisten. Cover; chill for several hours. To serve, place mushroom mixture on a lettuce-lined platter. Sprinkle with cheese and chives. Pass extra dressing.

DUXELLES

Makes about 3 cups

Duxelles is a minced mushroom and butter mixture that is cooked slowly until it becomes a thickened, reduced mass. This French classic is well worth having on hand. It will keep, refrigerated, for a week and can be frozen. Add to sauces, soups and dips. It is concentrated, so a small amount adds a generous jolt of flavor. Some recipes call for sautéing a bit of minced onion or garlic before adding the mushrooms.

$\frac{1}{2}$ cup butter
2 lb. fresh mushrooms with stems, finely chopped

In a large saucepan, melt butter, add mushrooms and lower heat. Cook, stirring occasionally, until mushrooms are cooked down and very dark. This takes about 30 minutes and should not be hurried.

MUSHROOM FUMET

Makes about 1 cup

*Fumet, pronounced "foo-MAY," is a concentrated
stock used as a base for sauces.*

½ lb. fresh mushrooms, chopped
3 tbs. butter
½ tsp. lemon juice
salt

Place mushrooms in a saucepan and just cover with water. Add
butter, lemon juice and salt. Bring to a boil, reduce heat and simmer
for 10 minutes. Strain and return liquid to pan. Continue to cook until
reduced by ⅓. Cool and refrigerate.

MUSHROOM STUFFING

Makes about 3 cups

Mushrooms add extra flavor to this simple stuffing. Use this to make a well-roasted chicken taste even better.

6 slices firm-textured white bread, crusts removed
6 green onions, thinly sliced
3 tbs. minced fresh parsley
10 large fresh mushrooms, coarsely chopped
1 stalk celery, thinly sliced
salt and pepper
¼ cup butter, melted

In a large bowl, combine bread, onions, parsley, mushrooms, celery, salt and pepper. Pour melted butter over mixture and toss gently to combine.

MUSHROOM SPOONBREAD

Servings 6-8

Enjoy this as a side dish with chicken or meat.

1 tbs. minced shallots
3 tbs. butter
½ lb. fresh mushrooms, coarsely chopped
½ tsp. dried thyme
2 cups milk
⅔ cup cornmeal
salt and pepper
¼ cup butter
4 egg yolks, lightly beaten
¼ cup freshly grated Parmesan cheese
6 egg whites

Preheat oven to 350°. In a large skillet, sauté shallots in 3 tbs. butter until soft. Add mushrooms and thyme and cook until pan juices evaporate.

In a saucepan, bring milk to a boil. Whisk in cornmeal, salt and pepper. Slowly beat in ¼ cup butter. Remove from heat; beat in egg yolks and Parmesan. Fold in mushroom mixture.

Beat egg whites until soft peaks form and fold into saucepan. Spoon mixture into a buttered 2-quart casserole dish and bake for 35 minutes or until brown and puffy.

MUSHROOM QUICK BREAD

Makes 3 small or 1 large loaf

*This light, moist, quickly prepared bread is perfect
with soup or salad.*

1 tbs. butter
¾ lb. fresh mushrooms, finely chopped
2 cloves garlic, minced
1½ cups all-purpose flour
1 tsp. baking powder
½ tsp. baking soda
½ tsp. salt
½ cup freshly grated Parmesan cheese
1 egg
¾ cup milk
3 tbs. butter, melted
¼ cup minced fresh parsley

Preheat oven to 325°. In a large skillet, melt 1 tbs. butter. Add mushrooms and garlic; cook, stirring, over medium heat until quite dry. Cool.

In a small bowl, combine flour, baking powder, baking soda, salt and cheese.

In a large bowl, whisk together egg, milk and 3 tbs. melted butter. Stir in mushroom mixture and parsley. Add flour mixture and mix just enough to combine.

Spoon into three lightly greased 6-x-3-x-2-inch loaf pans or one 9-x-5-x-3-inch loaf pan. Bake until a wooden skewer inserted in the center comes out clean. Cool on a rack for 5 minutes. Remove loaves from pans and cool completely.

MUSHROOM SANDWICH SPREAD

Makes about 1½ cups

This excellent sandwich filling is also delicious spread thickly on baguette rounds, placed under the broiler for 2 to 3 minutes and served hot as an appetizer.

¼ lb. fresh mushrooms, finely chopped
½ cup chopped black olives
2 green onions, thinly sliced
1 tbs. minced fresh parsley
1 tbs. lemon juice
3-4 tbs. mayonnaise

Mix all ingredients together. Refrigerate unused portion.

MUSHROOM-PEPPER GRATIN

Servings 4

This tasty dish pairs well with meat, poultry or fish.

3 tbs. butter
1½ lb. fresh mushrooms, thickly sliced
1 red bell pepper, seeded and thickly sliced
3 cloves garlic, minced
⅓ cup half-and-half
salt
freshly grated nutmeg
1 lb. russet potatoes, peeled and sliced ¼-inch thick

Preheat oven to 425°. In a skillet, melt butter. Sauté mushrooms, pepper and garlic until soft; remove vegetables with a slotted spoon. Set aside. Add half-and-half, salt and nutmeg to pan juices. In a buttered 1-quart casserole dish, layer potatoes and mushroom mixture, ending with potatoes. Pour pan juices over mixture and bake for 25 minutes or until potatoes are tender and browned on top.

SCALLOPED MUSHROOMS AND POTATOES

Servings 6

*An upscale version of good old scalloped potatoes,
this dish is perfect with a fall or winter meal.*

3 shallots, chopped
1 lb. fresh mushrooms, thickly sliced
3 tbs. olive oil
1 tsp. dried thyme
salt
3 tbs. minced fresh parsley
3 large russet potatoes, sliced ¼-inch thick
1 cup half-and-half
1 egg yolk

Preheat oven to 350°. In a large skillet, sauté shallots and mushrooms in olive oil until soft. Add thyme, salt and parsley. Mix well.

Blanch potato slices by placing in boiling water for 3 minutes; drain well. Lightly oil a shallow 1-quart baking dish and place ½ of the potato slices on the bottom. Cover with mushroom mixture and with remaining potatoes. In a small bowl, whisk together half-and-half and egg yolk and pour over potatoes. Cover with foil and bake for 45 minutes. Uncover, increase oven temperature to 450° and bake for 10 minutes or until top is golden.

POLISH BAKED MUSHROOMS

Servings 6

Serve this hearty side dish with meat or chicken.

¼ cup butter	1 tbs. all-purpose flour
¾ lb. fresh mushrooms, thinly sliced	2 tbs. freshly grated Parmesan cheese
1 tbs. minced onion	1 cup heavy cream
1 tbs. lemon juice	2 egg yolks, lightly beaten
salt and pepper	2 tbs. soft breadcrumbs

Preheat oven to 375°. Combine butter, mushrooms and onion in a large skillet. Sprinkle with lemon juice, cover tightly and simmer for 3 minutes. Add salt and pepper and stir in flour and cheese. Mix well. Cook for 3 minutes. Transfer to a shallow 1-quart baking dish. Beat cream and egg yolks; pour over mushroom mixture. Sprinkle with breadcrumbs. Bake for 15 minutes or until bubbly and browned.

MUSHROOM KUGEL

Servings 4

*Kugel is a baked pudding traditionally served
on the Jewish Sabbath.*

1 tbs. canola oil	1 tbs. lemon juice
⅔ lb. fresh mushrooms, coarsely chopped	1 cup small curd cottage cheese
½ onion, finely chopped	3 tbs. minced fresh parsley
½ red bell pepper, seeded and finely chopped	salt and pepper
	6 oz. medium-wide noodles, cooked and drained

Preheat oven to 350°. Heat oil in a medium skillet. Add mushrooms, onion and red pepper. Sprinkle with lemon juice and sauté until vegetables are soft. Remove to a bowl and combine with cottage cheese, parsley, salt, pepper and noodles. Spoon into a lightly oiled 1-quart casserole dish and bake for 30 minutes. Serve warm.

MUSHROOM PUDDING

Servings 4

Use a casserole or soufflé dish for this savory side dish.

¼ cup butter
1 lb. fresh mushrooms, finely
  chopped
2 tbs. finely chopped onion

2 tbs. all-purpose flour
2 eggs, separated
½ cup half-and-half
salt and pepper

Preheat oven to 350°. In a large skillet, melt butter and sauté mushrooms and onion until quite a bit of liquid is released from mushrooms. Remove mushrooms and set aside. Add flour to mushroom liquid and cook until thickened; beat egg yolks with half-and-half and whisk in. Add mushrooms, salt and pepper to sauce; beat egg whites until soft peaks form and fold in. Spoon mixture into a buttered 1-quart dish and bake for 30 to 40 minutes until cooked in the center and nicely browned on top.

WILD RICE AND MUSHROOMS

Servings 4-6

A selection of wild mushrooms is perfect with wild rice, but if only white buttons are available, this dish will still be good.

¼ cup butter, divided
1 bunch green onions, finely
  chopped, including greens
1 cup wild rice

2 cups chicken stock
½ lb. fresh mushrooms, sliced
⅓ cup toasted pine nuts
salt and pepper

Preheat oven to 350°. In an ovenproof 1½-quart casserole dish, melt 2 tbs. butter and sauté onions until soft. Add wild rice and stock. Stir well, bring to a boil, cover and bake for 1 hour. Remove from oven and cool for 15 minutes. In a large skillet, melt remaining butter and sauté mushrooms until pan juices evaporate. Stir mushrooms, pine nuts, salt and pepper into rice.

RUSSIAN KASHA AND MUSHROOMS

Servings 6

Kasha, or buckwheat groats, is a delightfully different side dish. Top with a dollop of sour cream, if desired.

1 cup kasha
1 egg
1 tsp. salt
1 cup butter, divided

2-3 cups boiling water
2 cups finely chopped onion
1 lb. fresh mushrooms,
   coarsely chopped

In a large skillet, combine kasha and egg; stir over medium heat until kasha grains are separated. Add salt, 3 tbs. butter and 2 cups boiling water. Stir, cover, reduce heat and cook, stirring occasionally, for 20 minutes. If kasha is not tender but is dry, stir in 1 cup boiling water and cook until it is absorbed. In a large skillet, melt 3 tbs. butter and sauté onion until soft. Add to kasha. Melt remaining butter and sauté mushrooms until pan juices evaporate. Add to kasha and serve.

                         SAUCES AND SIDES

MUSHROOM STROGANOFF

Servings 4-6

Spinach adds a lot of flavor to this Old World meatless dish.

2 tbs. canola oil
1 onion, finely sliced
4 cloves garlic, minced
2 tsp. paprika
¼ tsp. freshly grated nutmeg
1 tsp. Worcestershire sauce
dash Tabasco Sauce

1 lb. fresh mushrooms, sliced
1 cup vegetable stock
8 cups shredded fresh spinach
1½ cups sour cream
salt
½-¾ lb. noodles, cooked and
    drained

In a skillet, heat oil and sauté onion and garlic until soft. Mix in seasonings; cook for 1 minute. Add mushrooms. Stir occasionally until quite dry. Add stock, bring to a boil, reduce heat and boil gently until liquid is reduced by ⅓. Mix in spinach; stir until just wilted. Blend in sour cream and salt. Heat through and serve over hot noodles.

MUSHROOM-BEEF STEW

Servings 4

*This intensely flavored dish is a wonderful do-ahead dinner.
Serve with noodles, rice or boiled new potatoes.*

4 oz. dried mushrooms
⅓ cup dry red wine, warmed
1 lb. lean stew beef
flour seasoned with salt and pepper
2 tbs. canola oil
1-1½ cups beef stock
1 cup coarsely chopped onions
sour cream, optional

Soak mushrooms in red wine for 30 minutes. Strain through a paper coffee filter; reserve wine. Rinse mushrooms, squeeze dry, chop coarsely, return to wine and set aside.

Cut meat into ½-inch cubes and dredge in seasoned flour, shaking off excess. Preheat oven to 350°. In a large skillet, brown meat in oil; transfer to a 1-quart ovenproof dish. Pour ¾ cup beef stock into skillet and cook over high heat, scraping pan to loosen browned bits; pour pan drippings over meat. Cover and place in oven.

Check after 30 minutes and add more stock, if needed. After 1 hour, add onions and cook for 30 minutes. Add mushrooms and wine and cook for 15 minutes. Most of the liquid should be absorbed at the end of cooking. If too much remains, reduce, uncovered, over high heat on top of stove. Serve with sour cream, if desired.

MUSHROOM RAGOÛT

Servings 4

Ragoût is a French word for a rich, seasoned stew. In this dish, several types of mushrooms, both fresh and dried, are essential for a full and robust flavor. It is especially good with polenta, but also try it with pasta or chicken.

⅔ cup beef stock, heated
4 oz. dried mushrooms
1 onion, finely chopped
3 cloves garlic, minced
2 tbs. olive oil
1 tsp. dried oregano
¾ lb. fresh mushrooms, thinly sliced
½ cup dry red wine
dash Tabasco Sauce

In a small bowl, pour beef stock over dried mushrooms and soak for 30 minutes. Strain through a paper coffee filter, reserving liquid. Rinse mushrooms, squeeze dry and chop coarsely, discarding tough stems.

In a large skillet, sauté onion and garlic in olive oil until soft. Add oregano and fresh mushrooms and cook until almost dry. Add dried mushrooms. Combine strained beef stock, red wine and Tabasco and add to mushroom mixture. Bring to a boil, reduce heat and simmer until reduced to desired consistency.

MUSHROOM-SAUSAGE PUDDING

Servings 6-8

This superb entrée is also perfect as a brunch dish.
It must be prepared the night before.

2-3 tbs. butter, softened
12 slices white bread (preferably sourdough), crusts removed
$\frac{1}{4}$ cup butter
$\frac{1}{2}$ lb. fresh mushrooms, thickly sliced
2 cups thinly sliced onion
$1\frac{1}{2}$ lb. sweet Italian sausage, casing removed
1 lb. sharp cheddar cheese, grated
5 eggs
$2\frac{1}{2}$ cups milk
3 tbs. Dijon mustard
2 tbs. minced fresh parsley

Spread softened butter on bread and set aside. In a large skillet, heat ¼ cup butter and sauté mushrooms and onion until soft and quite dry. Cut sausage into bite-sized pieces, cook until well done and drain well. In a lightly oiled 9-x-13-inch baking dish, layer half of the bread, mushroom-onion mixture, sausage and cheese. Repeat, ending with cheese. Mix remaining ingredients and pour over bread mixture. Cover and refrigerate overnight. To serve, preheat oven to 350°. Bring pudding to room temperature and bake for 1 hour.

POT ROAST WITH MUSHROOMS

Servings 4-6

Cook this in a heavy casserole dish with a tight-fitting lid.

1 tbs. butter
1 tbs. canola oil
4 lb. chuck roast, trimmed well
2 lb. fresh mushrooms, sliced

1 onion, stuck with 3 cloves
salt and pepper
dry white wine, as needed
½ cup sour cream

Preheat oven to 250°. Heat butter and oil in a heavy casserole dish and brown meat well on all sides. Add mushrooms and onion; cook over high heat for 2 minutes. Add salt and pepper; cover. Cook in oven for 2 to 3 hours or until meat is very tender. Mushrooms should provide enough liquid, but if they do not, add wine to keep contents moist. When meat is done, remove to a platter, slice and keep warm. Add sour cream to casserole dish; cook over high heat for 3 to 4 minutes to thicken slightly. Pour over meat.

TURKEY-MUSHROOM LOAF

Servings 4-6

This delectable turkey loaf may also be made with beef.

1 tbs. canola oil
½ lb. fresh mushrooms, finely
  chopped
1 lb. ground turkey
1 onion, finely chopped
2 cloves garlic, minced
1-2 jalapeño peppers, seeded
  and minced

½ tsp. chili powder
½ tsp. dried oregano
1 tsp. lemon juice
salt and pepper
1 egg, lightly beaten
1 cup crushed unseasoned
  corn chips

Preheat oven to 350°. In a small skillet, heat oil and sauté mushrooms until quite dry. In a large bowl, combine all ingredients and mix well. Shape into a loaf; place on a lightly oiled ovenproof plate. Bake for 1 hour. Allow to rest for a few minutes before slicing.

CHICKEN BREASTS SMOTHERED IN MUSHROOMS

Servings 4

This simple dish can be made ahead and reheated. Use frozen pearl onions, slightly thawed, for their uniform size.

4 oz. dried mushrooms
¾ cup dry white wine, warmed
¼ cup butter, divided, or more as needed
½ lb. fresh mushrooms, sliced
1½ cups pearl onions
4 half chicken breasts, boned and skinned
½ tsp. dried tarragon
salt

In a small bowl, soak dried mushrooms in wine for 30 minutes. Strain through a paper coffee filter, reserving ½ cup liquid. Chop mushrooms coarsely, discarding tough stems. Preheat oven to 350°.

In a large skillet, sauté soaked mushrooms in 1 tbs. butter for 3 minutes. Remove mushrooms and set aside. Add fresh mushrooms and more butter as needed and sauté until quite dry. Remove mushrooms and set aside. Add onions to skillet and more butter as needed and sauté for 5 minutes. Remove onions and set aside. Add chicken to skillet and more butter as needed and brown quickly on both sides.

Place chicken in a 1-quart casserole dish. "Smother" it with mushrooms and onions. Add reserved ½ cup mushroom soaking liquid, tarragon and salt to skillet; cook over high heat, scraping pan to loosen browned bits. Add to casserole, cover with a tight-fitting lid and bake for 20 minutes.

VEAL (OR CHICKEN) AND MUSHROOM BOREKS

Servings 6

Boreks are Turkish turnovers traditionally made with filo dough.

1 tbs. butter
1 large onion, minced
¾ lb. fresh mushrooms, finely chopped
1 lb. ground veal or chicken
salt and pepper
1 tsp. ground cumin
2 cloves garlic, minced
2 tbs. minced fresh parsley
½ cup grated Parmesan cheese
1 pkg. (10 oz.) frozen puff pastry shells, thawed

Melt butter in a large skillet and sauté onion until soft. Add mushrooms and cook for 5 minutes. Add veal or chicken, salt, pepper, cumin and garlic and continue cooking until meat is just cooked. Remove from heat; stir in parsley and cheese. Cool.

On a lightly floured surface, roll pastry shells as thin as possible, forming flat circles. Divide filling among shells, fold over to form half-circles and pinch edges together tightly to seal. Chill for 30 minutes. Preheat oven to 425°. Place boreks on an ungreased baking sheet and bake for 20 to 25 minutes or until puffed and golden.

SALMON-MUSHROOM BAKE

Servings 4-6

This is a simple supper dish for a busy evening.

1 can (15 oz.) salmon
4 oz. small pasta shells
½ cup mayonnaise
1 tsp. fresh or dried dill
½ lb. fresh mushrooms, sliced
¼ cup sliced celery
2 green onions, sliced
3 small zucchini, coarsely grated and squeezed dry
¾ cup grated mozzarella cheese

Drain and flake salmon. Preheat oven to 350°. Cook pasta shells and drain well. In a large bowl, combine salmon, shells, mayonnaise, dill, mushrooms, celery, green onions and zucchini. Spoon mixture into a 1-quart casserole dish and top with grated cheese. Bake for 20 minutes or until bubbly.

FETTUCCINI WITH MUSHROOMS AND ZUCCHINI

Servings 6

Pasta never tasted better than it does in this great dish.

½ lb. fresh mushrooms, thinly sliced
¼ cup butter
1½ lb. zucchini, grated and squeezed dry
1 cup half-and-half
¼ cup butter, cut in pieces
1½ lb. fettuccini, cooked and drained
¾ cup freshly grated Parmesan cheese
½ cup minced fresh parsley

In a large skillet, sauté mushrooms in ¼ cup butter for 2 minutes. Add zucchini, half-and-half and ¼ cup butter; bring to a boil, reduce heat and simmer for 3 minutes. Add fettuccini, cheese and parsley. Toss to combine well and transfer to a warm platter.

MUSHROOM LASAGNA

Servings 6

Everyone likes lasagna, and mushroom fanciers will love this.

SAUCE

1 oz. dried mushrooms
1 cup hot water
1½ tbs. olive oil
½ onion, finely chopped
¾ lb. fresh mushrooms, sliced

3 cloves garlic, minced
½ tsp. dried oregano
¼ cup dry red wine
1 can (15 oz.) whole tomatoes,
  chopped, with liquid

FILLING

15 oz. ricotta cheese
¼ cup freshly grated Parmesan
  cheese

¼ cup minced fresh parsley
1 egg
salt

about 10 lasagna noodles
8 oz. mozzarella cheese, sliced

To make sauce: Place dried mushrooms in a small bowl and cover with hot water. Allow to stand for 30 minutes. Drain through a paper coffee filter, reserving liquid. Rinse dried mushrooms, squeeze dry and chop, discarding any tough stems. Heat oil in a medium skillet and sauté onion until soft. Add dried and fresh mushrooms and garlic. Sauté for 5 minutes. Stir frequently. Add oregano, wine, reserved liquid and tomatoes. Boil to reduce liquid by half, reduce heat and simmer for 20 minutes.

To make filling: Combine all ingredients, mixing well.

Preheat oven to 350°. Cook noodles in a pot of boiling water until just tender. Place in a colander, rinse with cold water and drain well. Lightly oil an 8- or 9-inch square pan. Start with a layer of sauce. Follow with noodles, filling and mozzarella. Fill pan in this order, ending with cheese. Cover with foil and bake for 35 minutes. Uncover and continue baking for 30 minutes. Cool for 10 minutes.

MUSHROOM RAVIOLI EN BRODO

Makes 28 large ravioli

These generously sized ravioli, easily made with won ton wrappers, are an excellent first course or light meal when served Italian-style, "en brodo," which literally means "in broth."

FILLING

3 tbs. olive oil
½ onion, minced
2 cloves garlic, minced
1½ lb. fresh mushrooms, coarsely chopped
3 tbs. minced fresh parsley
½ cup dry white wine
1 tbs. dry breadcrumbs
1 tsp. lemon juice
salt

1 pkg. (48) won ton wrappers
1 egg white, beaten until foamy
2 qt. chicken stock

To make filling: In a medium skillet, heat oil and sauté onion and garlic until soft. Add mushrooms and sauté until soft. Stir in parsley and wine and continue cooking until mixture is quite dry. Add bread-crumbs, lemon juice and salt. Cool.

Arrange ½ of the won ton wrappers on lightly floured trays. Place a spoonful of filling in the center of each. Brush around the edges with egg white, top with a second wrapper and press edges together securely with the tines of a fork.

In a large pot, bring chicken stock to a boil. Add half of the ravioli, reduce heat and simmer gently for 3 to 5 minutes. Remove ravioli and a little stock to heated soup plates. Cook remaining ravioli. Add ravioli and more hot stock to soup plates and serve.

LEEK AND MUSHROOM QUICHE

Makes one 9-inch deep dish pie

This quiche is bursting with goodies.

2 tbs. canola oil
½ lb. fresh mushrooms, sliced
3 leeks, white part only, sliced
1 red bell pepper, seeded and
  finely chopped

one 9-inch deep dish pie crust,
  unbaked
¾ cup grated Swiss cheese
1½ cups half-and-half
3 large eggs

Preheat oven to 450°. In a skillet, heat oil and sauté mushrooms, leeks and red pepper until vegetables are limp and liquid evaporates. Cool slightly; transfer to pie crust. Cover with grated cheese; whisk together half-and-half and eggs and pour over cheese. Place on a baking sheet in oven for 12 minutes. Reduce heat to 300° and continue baking until a toothpick inserted in the center comes out clean, about 35 minutes. Cool slightly before serving.

MUSHROOM QUICHE CRUST

Makes one 9-inch crust

This unusual crust will make your favorite quiche better than ever.

3 tbs. butter
½ lb. fresh mushrooms, finely chopped
⅓ cup fine dry breadcrumbs
2 tbs. wheat germ

In a large skillet, melt butter and sauté mushrooms until limp. Remove from heat and stir in breadcrumbs and wheat germ. Spoon into a well-oiled 9-inch quiche dish or pie plate, and press mixture evenly into the bottom and up the sides.

CREPES À L'ARDENNAISE

Servings 4-6

For the crepes, be sure to use granular flour, which can be found in any supermarket. "À l'ardennaise" means "of the Ardennes," a region in France near Champagne, bordering on Belgium.

12 *Basic Crepes*, recipe follows
1 tbs. butter
½ lb. fresh mushrooms, finely chopped
2 shallots, minced
2 cloves garlic, minced

2 cups half-and-half, divided
½ lb. cooked ham, finely chopped
salt and pepper
½ cup grated Swiss cheese

Prepare *Basic Crepes* and set aside. In a medium skillet, melt butter and sauté mushrooms, shallots and garlic until liquid evaporates. Add a tablespoon or two of half-and-half, ham, salt and pepper. Preheat oven to 350°. Cook filling mixture over low heat for 15 minutes, stirring frequently. Divide filling among 12 crepes, roll each one and place, seam down, in a shallow baking dish. Pour remaining half-and-half over and top with cheese. Cover with foil and bake for 20 minutes. Remove foil and place under broiler to brown lightly.

BASIC CREPES

1 cup cold water
1 cup cold milk
4 eggs, large
½ tsp. salt
¼ cup butter, melted
1½ cups granular flour

With a whisk, slowly blend water, milk, eggs, salt and butter into flour. When smooth, cook in a lightly buttered skillet over medium-high heat. When crepes are light brown on the bottom, turn to cook other side. Cool on a rack. Use immediately or stack between pieces of waxed paper to freeze. Makes twenty 6-inch crepes.

MUSHROOM-ONION DUTCH BABY

Servings 4

The presentation of this dish is spectacular.

5 tbs. butter, divided
½ lb. fresh mushroom, thinly
  sliced
1 small onion, minced
4 eggs

¼ tsp. freshly grated nutmeg
1 cup milk
1 cup flour
⅓ cup finely grated Swiss
  cheese

Preheat oven to 425°. In a 10- or 11-inch skillet with an ovenproof handle, melt 3 tbs. butter. Add mushrooms and onion; sauté until pan juices evaporate. Add remaining butter. In a small bowl, beat eggs with nutmeg. Add milk and continue beating. Beat in flour; set aside.

Place skillet in oven. When butter is melted, pour egg mixture over mushrooms. Sprinkle with cheese, return to oven and bake for 20 to 25 minutes or until puffy and browned. Serve immediately.

INDEX